Cheshire
Edited by Claire Tupholme

 Young **Writers**
First published in Great Britain in 2008 by:
Young Writers
Remus House
Coltsfoot Drive
Peterborough
PE2 9JX
Telephone: 01733 890066
Website: www.youngwriters.co.uk

All Rights Reserved

© *Copyright Contributors 2008*

SB ISBN 978-1 84431 677 9

Foreword

Young Writers was established in 1991 and has been passionately devoted to the promotion of reading and writing in children and young adults ever since. The quest continues today. Young Writers remains as committed to the nurturing of poetic and literary talent as ever.

This year's Young Writers competition has proven as vibrant and dynamic as ever and we are delighted to present a showcase of the best poetry from across the UK and in some cases overseas. Each poem has been selected from a wealth of *Little Laureates 2008* entries before ultimately being published in this, our seventeenth primary school poetry series.

Once again, we have been supremely impressed by the overall quality of the entries we have received. The imagination, energy and creativity which has gone into each young writer's entry made choosing the poems a challenging and often difficult but ultimately hugely rewarding task - the general high standard of the work submitted ensured this opportunity to bring their poetry to a larger appreciative audience.

We sincerely hope you are pleased with this final collection and that you will enjoy *Little Laureates 2008 Cheshire* for many years to come.

Contents

Bredbury Green Primary School

Matthew Hopkins (9)	1
James Howe (9)	1
Callum Gee (10)	2
Henry Dippnall (10)	2
Henry Dippnall (10)	3
Daniel Lees (10)	3
Ashley Harper (10)	4
Gianni Paolucci (9)	4
Josh Clarke (10)	5
Franceska Gage (9)	5
Hayley Farrell (10)	6
Hannah Doyle (10)	6
Kirsty Evans (9)	7
Amy Hayes (10)	7
Poppy Howells (10)	8
Amy Allen (9)	8
Ben Ayre (9)	9
Ryan Babcock (10)	9
Natasha Sands (9)	10
Rachael Burgess (10)	10
Jack Walker (10)	11

Calveley Primary School

Ross Wild (9)	11
Elizabeth Brunt (9)	12
Joab Huntbach (8)	12
James White (8)	13

Eaton Primary School

Katy Oakeshott (8)	13
Cassine Bering (11)	14
Theo Hesketh (7)	14
Jack Martell (8)	15
Ryan Watson (9)	15
Heather Sheldon (7)	16
Jordan Gaskell (8)	16

Jasmine Appleton (8)	17
Mark Latham (9)	17
Frances Hurst (8)	18
Harry Moore (9)	18

Grange Community Primary School

Emily Gannon (9)	19
Michael Flood (9)	19
Karl Morgan (10)	20
Courtney Massey (10)	20
Jordan Fairfield (10)	21
Jack McKenzie (10)	21
Jasmine Sugarman (9)	22
Joshua Moore (10)	23
Lewis Parry (9)	24
Owen Birtles (9)	24
Rebecca Twigg (10)	25

Hazel Grove Primary School

Alana Peebles (10)	25
Amy Kenyon (10)	25
Andrew Johnson-Hill (10)	26
Louisa Wood (10)	26
Luke Burgess (11)	27
Rosie Spedding (10)	27
Mike Wild (11)	28
Callum Spencer (10)	28
Danielle Massey (10)	28
Hollie Hatton (11)	29
Zunnur Choudhury (11)	29
Bryony Ingham Tatton (10)	29
Jessica Perry (11)	30
Georgia Greaves (10)	30
Nicholas Church (11)	30
Niamh Clarke (10)	31
Tonicha Blackwell (11)	31
Jessica Elwers (11)	31
Megan Pickford (11)	32
Moses Silweya (10)	32
Luke Ingham (10)	33
Brandon Forsyth (10)	33

Elizabeth Parrott (11)	34
Chloe Hall (10)	34
Lucy Potter (10)	34
Emily Barnett (10)	35
Katherine Parrott (11)	35
Ashby Nelson (10)	35

Hursthead Junior School

Hattie Brooks-Davies (11)	36
Eloise Jepson (8)	36
Alice Godridge (9)	37
Grace Byrne (10)	37
Lauren Sampson (7)	38
Holly Henderson (8)	38
Mya Mannion (10)	39
Mya Bhatt (10)	39
Hannah Steele (9)	40
Jenny Bartlett (9)	41
Alex Benton (8)	42
Hannah Hughes (8)	42
Luke Fallon (8)	43
Rachael Casnello (8)	43
Grace Mannion (8)	44
Isabella Hargreaves Cronshaw (8)	44
James McElhone (11)	45
Alice Casnello (10)	45
Kirsten Williams-Lee (9)	46
Alexandra Templeman (8)	46
Lucy Godridge (11)	47
Sophie Holt (9)	47
Jessica Lucas (8)	48

Lime Tree Primary School

Jessica Murray (10)	49
Lucie Lyth (11)	49
Lewis Bright (10)	49
Georgia Taylor (11)	50
Christopher Harris (10)	50
Premtim Bujupi (11)	50
Sahara Roberts (11)	51
Katie Baddoo (11)	51

Benjamin Hartley (11)   51
Jake Robertson (10)   52
Callum Lownds (10)   52
Heather Watts (10)   52

Newton Primary School
Chloe Elsom (11)   53
Lucy Kelly (10)   53
Beth Bolton (11)   54
Samantha Brockhurst (10)   54
Saskia Steels-Wright (11)   55

Oldfield Brow Primary School
Amy Wooller (8)   55
Russell Henstock (8)   56
Jade Taylor (8)   56
Sophie Warmisham (8)   57
Ahmad Arshad (8)   57
Sophie Brown (10)   58
Rhys Gregory (8)   58
Tamzin Ogiliev (8)   59
Simal Asher (9)   60
Deniz Koncagul (8)   61
Shannon Howell (8)   62
James Telford (8)   63
Jessica Tandy (8)   64
Erica Dook (9)   65

Our Lady's Catholic Primary School
Emma-Louise Tweedale (7)   65
James Toner (8)   66
Chloe Toner (11)   66
Victoria Campbell (9)   67
Alicia Cheeseman (8)   67
Grace Crosthwaite (8)   68
Eleanor Henderson (11)   68
Niamh Crowley (9)   69
Alicia Blythe (8)   69
Toni-Marie Tweedale (11)   70

St Ambrose RC Primary School, Stockport
Jamie Morris (10)	70
Adam Bircher (10)	71
Abigail Jackson (11)	72
Dominic Chase (11)	72
Michael Lynam (10)	73
Jessica Lewis (8) & Kelly Wong (9)	73
Thomas Reeves (10)	74
Daniel Keeble (11)	74
Alex Worthington (8)	75
Lucy Sharpe (8)	75
Jamie Bentley (8)	75
Megan Toombs (8)	76

St Lewis Catholic Primary School, Croft
Rose Byrne (10)	76
Kaysey Reddecliff (7)	77
Benjamin Hutson-Redfearn (7)	77
Georgia Hatton (8)	77
Gabrielle Healey (10)	78
Connor Beck (9)	78
Gregor Nolan (10)	79
Sinead Wright (10)	79
Joe Burnham & Liam (8)	80
Daisy & Maddy Howorth (7)	80
Kate Duncombe (8)	80
Katie Janes (9)	81

Winsford High Street CP School
Benjamin Jackson (9)	81
Charlotte Jones (8)	82
Laura Stobie (9)	82
Brenden Macken (9)	82
Jessica Davies (8)	83
Robyn Bettley (9)	83
Cameron Atherton (8)	83
Reiss Bratt (10)	84
Sophie Buckley (9)	84
Imogen Graffham (9)	84
Shola Hornby (9)	85
Georgia Kittle (9)	85

Harry Fairweather (9)	85
Crailin Wilson (10)	86
Jason Wilshaw (10)	86
Alexander Gaucas Noden (9)	86
Becky Wilson (10)	87
Lauren Tomlinson (10)	87
Chloe Walton (9)	87
Toyah-Ann Thelwell (9)	88
Aiden Sharratt (9)	88
Kyle Reece-Lea (8)	88
Ellie Motherwell (8)	88
Emily Hall (8)	89
James Maddock (8)	89
Emily Goodier (7)	89
Ben Kent (9)	89
Alasdair Smith (9)	90
Jessica Hulse (9)	90
Hannah Wenborn (9)	91
Alexandra Butler (10)	91
Eleanor Dale (9)	92
Jake Noble (8)	92
Matthew Warburton (10)	92
Joshua Graves (9)	93
Bradley Perrin (9)	93
Adam Blackburn (9)	93
Sophie Duncan (10)	94
Emma Galley (10)	94
Reyce Heath (10)	95
Layla Rigby (9)	95
Joshua Rosenberg (10)	96
Callum Coggin (9)	96
Caitlin Casselden (9)	96

Wrenbury Primary School

Amelia Penn (10)	97
Amy Hill (9)	97
Hayley Harman (11)	98
Ted Shakeshaft (10)	99
Jemima Crawley (10)	100
David Rowley (9)	101
Joe Mason (10)	102

Amy Hickman (10)	103
Jodie Ann Hill (9)	104
Bradley Williams (9)	104
Philippa Eite (10)	105
Nathaniel Macleod (9)	105
Callum Bourne (9)	106
Ben Woodward (9)	107

The Poems

Should I Tell?

I go in school and wait for him,
But the school fire alarm goes off.
Is there a real fire? I look around; no, it's *him*.
He picks me up by my collar and
Pushes me into the wall,
He punches me, he drops me;
I fall, left stranded there and beaten up.
The teacher sees me and helps me up like a fireman would.
He asks me, 'Did you see anyone set off the alarm?'
I look around, I see him attacking other kids.
I say, 'Yes,' and fall.

Matthew Hopkins (9)
Bredbury Green Primary School

The Innocent

I am here all alone waiting,
I am waiting for the day,
The day I get killed,
Or maybe I'll decay.

In a cold and dusty cell,
Trapped and all alone,
Listening to the death cries
And the occasional groan.

I was not guilty, not me,
The court told me I was going to die.
I protested, none listened,
But when I'm gone, oh how they will cry.

James Howe (9)
Bredbury Green Primary School

Global Warming

Planet Earth is blue and green,
The rubbish and waste
Is not a good taste,

Global warming.

It needs to stop before it gets a lot,
The gas and fumes make you cough.

It's really not a nice sight,
It looks like a house after a fight.

Please help the world for me and for you
And the entire human race.

This isn't a joke, it's really serious.
Stop!

Global warming.

Callum Gee (10)
Bredbury Green Primary School

Don't Dump The Lot

Don't turn the sky grey, turn it light blue.
Don't turn the sea brown, turn it turquoise.
Don't turn the ground black, turn it green.
Don't turn the air to smoke, turn it clean.
Don't put the animals to death, let them live.
Don't kill the trees dead, plant many more.
Don't kill the light.
Don't kill ourselves.
Don't kill the Earth.

Henry Dippnall (10)
Bredbury Green Primary School

Don't Dump The Lot

Don't turn the sky grey, turn it light blue.
Don't turn the sea brown, turn it turquoise.
Don't turn the ground black, turn it green.
Don't turn the air to smoke, turn it clean.
Don't put the animals to death, let them live.
Don't kill the trees dead, plant many more.
Don't kill the light.
Don't kill ourselves.
Don't kill the Earth.

Henry Dippnall (10)
Bredbury Green Primary School

Stop Right Now

There is too much pollution,
It is all because of us,
We all drive cars,
Please think and go on a bus.

Are you watching the TV?
Well this is a warning,
Stop right now,
You're creating global warming.

Stop right now,
You're creating smoke,
Please stop and think,
You are treating it like a joke.

Cough, cough, cough, cough,
The oxygen is getting mucky.
There is too much pollution,
The world is just not lucky.

Daniel Lees (10)
Bredbury Green Primary School

Pollution Everywhere

There's rubbish on the pavement,
There are wrappings on the floor,
There's pollution in the air
And we don't want more.

There's chewing gum everywhere,
There is waste being dumped,
We need to make the environment green,
Our towns are being slumped.

Oxygen makes you cough,
There's gas in the air,
There's lots of petrol lying around,
Pollution is everywhere.

There's burnt wood in the park,
We need to save every plant.
There's lots of fuel left around,
And that's my cool, cool chant.

Ashley Harper (10)
Bredbury Green Primary School

The Grey Planet

The Earth is dying, dirt is falling,
We are killing everything.
It's going to waste, in no form or shape,
Save the Earth, she's helpless.

Plants dying, smoke spreading,
It's our fault, not hers.
Carbon dioxide, helium, it's ruining all,
Save the Earth, she's helpless.

It's getting worse,
There's nothing we can do,
Is there?

Gianni Paolucci (9)
Bredbury Green Primary School

Stop Environmental Pollution

Rubbish on the streets,
Rubbish at my door,
Rubbish at my window,
Rubbish we abhor.

Cans in the street,
Cans in my pocket,
Cans in my bike shelter,
We have got to stop it.

Leaves on the trees,
Leaves in my hair,
Leaves in the sewers,
Leaves everywhere.

Gum in my house,
Gum on my bike,
Gum on my fence,
Gum on my trike.

Pollution here,
Pollution there,
Pollution where?
Pollution everywhere.

Josh Clarke (10)
Bredbury Green Primary School

A Life On the Street

On the street everyone is mean to me
Because I am not clean.
I feed myself out of bins
And drink out of tins.

I will walk the street
But everyone will beep at me.
I would try and meet people
But they would laugh at me.
I belong in the dump, rubbish, rubbish.

Franceska Gage (9)
Bredbury Green Primary School

Stop And Look

The trees are dying,
The plants are dead,
It's all because of this pollution spread.

How could we do this?
Just stop and look,
Can you not see what we all took?

Go on a scooter,
Go on a bike,
Anything will do,
Go on a hike.

Are you driving your car?
Well listen to this,
You're giving global warming a big death kiss!

If you go to the beach,
Don't throw rubbish on the floor,
Put it in the bins that are by the door.

Hayley Farrell (10)
Bredbury Green Primary School

Our Planet Earth

Our planet Earth
Is so ill,
Killing it with pollution,
There is no pill.
Emissions from light,
Hot rays from the sun,
Forgetting to recycle,
This is no fun!

Hannah Doyle (10)
Bredbury Green Primary School

Help!

This planet used to be a wonderful place,
We never really knew what it meant.

The trees and plants blow in the wind,
We used to laugh and dance and sing.

These people are doing their best to stop
All the pollution before we drop.

Maybe we can help save us all,
We never used to care at all.

Kirsty Evans (9)
Bredbury Green Primary School

The World

Plants are pretty
And they're everywhere.
You can feel the wind
But you can't see the air.

I like the trees
When they sway,
So come over here
And watch them today.

When it is sunny
The birds all sing
And when it is windy
All the chimes ring.

The sky is blue,
The sea is too,
Come over here
And I'll show you.

Amy Hayes (10)
Bredbury Green Primary School

Save The Environment

The environment is in danger,
The plants need more soil,
Everywhere is rubbish
And the nasty thing is oil.

The thing that splatters on the floor is rain,
Don't use too much paper or you're not saving the trees.
The trees make oxygen,
Open the good environment with the keys to a new start.

Everywhere around you is your environment,
But nearly everything is dead.
Stop litter, litter, litter,
Please stop pollution spread.

Waste gets dug into the ground,
They don't care that everything is bare.
The air is a horrible thing with pollution in it,
Nobody cares!

Poppy Howells (10)
Bredbury Green Primary School

The Last Disaster

Monday, I went to the sea.
Tuesday, it went brown.
Wednesday, I went to the tip.
Thursday, there was no space left.
Friday, I went to pick apples.
Saturday, the tree wasn't there.
Sunday, the planet was wrecked
And the dirty, disgusting disease spread.

Amy Allen (9)
Bredbury Green Primary School

Pollution Destroys

Trees show clean and nice new green,
Don't chop them down, reuse.

The blue is black because of oil,
The green looks grey because of exhaust fumes.
Now there's hardly any sun because of all the horrible smog.
The ice goes from white to grey to nasty blue, then to black.
Why?
Ice, dirt, nasty polluted water.

Greys, blacks, no blues and greens,
Make it stop or die under fumes.

Ben Ayre (9)
Bredbury Green Primary School

End Of The World

Cars make grey, trees make green,
Mix them together
And you make doom.

Flowers are bright like the moon in the night,
But now they are not,
Because of what?

Maybe you will stop your car
And find out what you are.

Outside in the air people are smelling something
But they don't know why they are dying.
Is it the poison?
They don't even care,
I might die anywhere.

Ryan Babcock (10)
Bredbury Green Primary School

Damaged Earth

The beautiful Earth lay there in space,
The jewelled green and crystal blue.
Then something happened to the place,
The blue changed colour but who knew?

The flowers and trees were killed,
The air turned to smoke,
The wind was milled
And everything was soaked.

The green went away
And everything was destroyed,
The people had nothing to say,
But God got annoyed.

Oh no, what happened?

Natasha Sands (9)
Bredbury Green Primary School

Dirty Environment

When the flowers get their powers
They suddenly start to die.
Just seeing them doing something like that,
It makes me want to cry.

The water in the river was blue,
But then it started to change.
The colours turned into mud,
It even began to smell strange!

The air was very fresh and clean,
But then it suddenly turned awful.
It went all dirty and you couldn't breathe,
People, animals, our plants and trees.

Rachael Burgess (10)
Bredbury Green Primary School

World Disaster

The sky is brown, the sea is green,
We have let you down.
It is chaos down here.
The smoke is coming,
Stop running.

Just stop running and try recycling,
Try to make the sea and sky blue again.
Make the world well again, please.
Stop ruining it, make it a better place.

Jack Walker (10)
Bredbury Green Primary School

My Family!

Dear sweetie-pie Mum,
Don't be glum
Cos you've got a number one son,
Who's lots and lots of fun.

Dear old Dad,
Don't be sad,
Cos you look very glad
That Mum isn't mad.
I bet she'd let you go to the pub
And fill your tummy with lots of grub,
Or we could go to the park
To play on the wooden ark.

My brother is a nutter
And he makes me laugh when we have a bath.
I love him to bits,
But I don't like him when he passes me nits!

I have two rabbits called Flopsy and Ruby,
And two fat cats called Holly and Suki.
My rabbits annoy me when they scratch me a lot,
The cats like to snuggle up nice and hot.

Ross Wild (9)
Calveley Primary School

The Four Seasons

Winter
Winter is a cold time of year,
With snow all over the ground.
Christmas is in this cold time,
When Santa gives presents all around.

Spring
Spring is when the flowers come out
And all the bugs come too,
It starts to get a bit warmer as well
And people come over for a barbecue.

Summer
Summer is the warmest time,
When you can swim in the pool,
You can also go on holiday
And be relaxed and cool.

Autumn
In autumn it dies down cold again
And the leaves are on the floor,
We also have Bonfire Night
And when the fireworks go I want more.

Elizabeth Brunt (9)
Calveley Primary School

My Drums!

I have a set of drums
And I play them really loud.
My grandpa is a drummer
And it makes me really proud.

My mum thinks I rock
And that I am really cool.
Sometimes I think I'd like to show
All my friends at school.

Joab Huntbach (8)
Calveley Primary School

Motorbike Racing

The day I went there
I heard the four strokes drone,
The *boom* of the crash
And the Aprilia's groan.

Further round the track
I heard the screech of the bend,
The click of the gears
As they raced to the end.

What's that now?
The Suzuki's won,
What a surprise,
Now the race is done.

James White (8)
Calveley Primary School

Daffodils

In the golden, peaceful field,
The bright sun was shining in the sky,
A group of gentle fluttering daffodils on the ground,
Bobbing up and down in the cool breeze.

In the dark, calm forest,
The wind sighing in the air,
A group of swaying bright daffodils
Tossing their heads round and round.

By the rippling emerald lake,
The pattering rain poured down,
A family of golden love
Cuddled together in a big circle.

Katy Oakeshott (8)
Eaton Primary School

Families

Mums are like a mouse
scurrying around the house,
but they're not as quiet,
in fact they make quite a riot,
scurrying about the house.

Dads are just as bad,
but are even more mad.
They think they look cool
when they look like a fool,
when dads get ready to go out.

Sisters are worse than blisters,
horrible, nasty things.
When they want a favour,
they have good behaviour,
when sisters want something.

Families are clever,
there with you forever.
When you need a helping hand,
they'll be there on demand.
That's why families are clever!

Cassine Bering (11)
Eaton Primary School

Daffodils

In the beautiful gold meadow
The sun glazed over
The swaying dancers
That were smiling with joy.

By the edge of the pond, the gold flowers
Stood gazing at the bright sun.
The rain came down on the sparkling petals,
A group of daffodils swaying with the breeze.

Theo Hesketh (7)
Eaton Primary School

The Daffodils

In the meadow near the farm,
The sun blazed like a million stars
Towards a troop of disciplined soldiers,
That victoriously gazed towards the fiery sun.

By the edge of the river,
A breeze blew gently
Over a patch of golden people,
Swaying as if they felt the world spinning.

In winter, in the snowy white field
Snow tilted off an icy flower,
The rest woke up from a freezing sleep
Like children snowball fighting.

In the house back garden,
The rain was pouring heavily down.
As the daffodils started to droop,
It was like a group of weeping people.

In the back of the school playground,
The mist slowly shrouded around the brightness,
But when it cleared the treasure was revealed:
A family of gently cuddling daffodils.

Jack Martell (8)
Eaton Primary School

Daffodils

On a delightful emerald-green field,
A shining sun was grinning pleasantly.
Something disturbed me.
A golden troop of daffodils,
Fluttering their trumpets at me
As if the troop of gold knows me.

Ryan Watson (9)
Eaton Primary School

Here Come The Daffodils!

On the glimmering grass
The round, warm sun gazed softly
On a cuddled-up yellow and orange crowd of shining stars
That sweetly smiled at the sun above.

By the edge of the swirling blue pond
The thin, soft breeze flew past
The tips of the delicate daffodils,
Bobbing up and down in the rhythm of the wind.

Under a blossoming light pink tree
The rain falls down, with their petals protecting the daffodils,
Bobbing up and down as if their trumpets were umbrellas.

Heather Sheldon (7)
Eaton Primary School

Daffodils

In the beautiful green meadow
Under a king emerald tree,
The sun glowing yellow and orange
On a herd of daffodils
Surrounding the trunk,
Bowing down at the royal tree
When the wind blew.

Jordan Gaskell (8)
Eaton Primary School

Daffodils, Daffodils

In the rays of the red-hot sun,
Looking at me,
Gazing delicately
As the little flower waits,
Humming to the beat of the wind pushing and bouncing,
A daffodil weeping in a crowd full of angels,
That smiles like a child.
Love goes through the air
Making a friendly family full of yellow people.

Jasmine Appleton (8)
Eaton Primary School

The Field Of Daffodils

In the field beside the fence,
the bright sun shone above
the forest of daffodils
that hummed through the gust of wind.

By the edge of the storming road,
as the rain trickled, they hid their heads,
a group of determined soldiers
marching through the powerful wind.

Mark Latham (9)
Eaton Primary School

Daffodils

In an emerald meadow,
The sun dazzled peacefully
On a sea of gold
That happily swayed.

Beside a calm lake
The breeze hummed
On a troupe of yellowish dancers
That bobbed up and down gently.

Near an empty field
A bundle of colours
Sheltered from the rain,
Smiling happily.

In a forest of flowers
The mist slowly uncovered
A troupe of bold dancers
That huddled together like a family of love.

Frances Hurst (8)
Eaton Primary School

Golden Daffodils

By the side of a brown hedge were some daffodils.
The sun blazed on the golden flowers as they bobbed.
A group of sunny trumpets swayed in the light wind,
Like soldiers bowing to their queen.

Harry Moore (9)
Eaton Primary School

The Town

In the town it's bright, it's light
As the lights are turned on.

Women crowding around
To see the clothes on sale,
Like vultures rising for their prey.

Mannequins in the shop line up
Like soldiers ready to fight.

Noise coming from every corner
Like a baby crying.

Please be quiet,
Please be quiet,
Please be quiet.

It goes dark as the lights are turned off.
The mannequins drift back to sleep
As it goes dark.

The draughty wind makes a silent noise.

I'm scared,
I'm scared,
I'm scared.

Emily Gannon (9)
Grange Community Primary School

Home Poem

Screaming with laughter,
It was as loud as an elephant stomping.

Vibrating like a drill in the wall,
Snoring like a lion roaring.

Talking like a monkey squeaking.

Michael Flood (9)
Grange Community Primary School

In The Park

In the park a young boy sits in a corner quietly.
Dogs running like a madman running to win a race.
People screaming, running and shouting on slides and swings,
It is like a football match.
The swings were swinging like a blizzard hit them.
The fair was open, the scratching metal from the rides
Was like people tearing paper.
There was screaming and shouting as if there was a fire.
The sound of music went through people's ears in the park.
The little boy asked to go on a ride.
'Please say yes, please say yes, please say yes.'

Karl Morgan (10)
Grange Community Primary School

The Hot Park

In a relaxed park birds were singing
Like a choir at a wedding.

Owners stride across the hot fields with their dogs.
Owners look at their dogs as they pant
As they run after footballs.

Families having picnics around a dirty lake.
Swans duck their heads under the water to cool down.

A few children playing on rusty swings.
Children sway as they are dizzy off a roundabout.

Courtney Massey (10)
Grange Community Primary School

The Beach

It was a boiling hot day like the heater was right up,
The sea was as cold as freezing ice in a freezer.
Children started to make sandcastles
As dogs knocked them over.
Mum and Dad swam in the sea
As crabs bit their feet.
Children buried mums and dads under the sand.

Let me out.
Let me out.
Let me out.

It was windy like a fan turned right up,
Sand was blowing everywhere.
The sea was soaking everyone,
People dived under the umbrellas.
It was dark, people were running into each other.
Families were running after buses.

Wait for me.
Wait for me.
Wait for me.

Jordan Fairfield (10)
Grange Community Primary School

Classroom

I am working like a zombie,
Every other person is
Crowding around the teacher
And thinking and thinking and thinking.

The kids are sitting like
A mummy in a coffin.
Everyone is writing like a genius,
A genius, a genius.

Jack McKenzie (10)
Grange Community Primary School

The Sea

There is no sound, all you can hear is birds
Tweeting with aimless notes at the seashore.
They can let themselves go,
With the sea as blue as a sapphire on a beautiful necklace.

The soft waves let the buoys hardly move,
It is as calm as a classroom where children do their tests
And toddlers try to swim with all their hearts.

Waves move slower and slower in certainly no hurry to win a race
But still they go on without a care in the world.

Always listen, listen, listen, there would have been
Things you've missed, until . . .

The sea is as ruffled as a scrunched-up piece of paper,
It's as black as a beetle, nobody dares to swim.

The clouds are as grey as ever, waves are
Darting as fast as a runaway dog,
The sand is a dark cream colour in the stormy wind.

Images run through my mind like a race car
Flying through the finish line.

Everything goes quiet as I slowly wake.

Jasmine Sugarman (9)
Grange Community Primary School

Football

As Wayne Rooney kicks the
Bright yellow ball over the crossbar,
The ball is aiming towards me,
I stand.
It pauses in my hands.
I cheer and sit down,
Sit down,
Sit down.

The whistle blows for half-time,
We sing for our first goal.
I get a hot dog and a burger
With some chips and tomato sauce,
To enjoy the second half.

Everyone's watching and everyone's listening,
The stadium's full and most of all, it's fun.

Still 0-0,
We've got a penalty,
Ronaldo kicks,
What a goal.
The whistle blows.
We win,
We win,
We win.

Joshua Moore (10)
Grange Community Primary School

The Beach

At the beach you can feel the relaxed sand sweeping across
                                                     your back,
Children making the loudest noise as the world shakes.

Jellyfish sting like an electric eel stinging up the water,
Dolphins jumping like a child on a trampoline.

Children playing in the water as fish jet through their legs,
The children watch.

As it turns dark,
The sand and the water go to sleep.
Children say,
'Let's go home.
Let's go home.
Let's go home.'

Lewis Parry (9)
Grange Community Primary School

The Classroom

In a confident classroom the children
Were working like an over-wound computer.

People were thinking so hard
Their brains could pop out.

Let's go out.
Let's go out.
Let's go out.

People run around in excitement,
Screaming and shouting, having fun.

Time to go in.
Time to go in.
Time to go in.

Owen Birtles (9)
Grange Community Primary School

The Beach

The sand is like a flame as you zoom across it
Like crabs catching your feet.

People shivering in the freezing cold,
iceberg pool.

Children spraying their marvellous parents
On the sunbeds getting a tan.

A cool draught through the tall, tall trees
Cools me down,
Cools me down,
Cools me down.

Rebecca Twigg (10)
Grange Community Primary School

Anger

As scary as a black panther,
Black as the darkness,
Burnt tea cakes,
A thunderstorm,
An explosion in the middle of nowhere,
People dying unpeacefully.

Alana Peebles (10)
Hazel Grove Primary School

Love Poem

Love looks like two doves kissing.
Love is as pink as rosy cheeks.
Love smells like freshly-cooked bread.
Love feels like a butterfly flying gracefully.
Love sounds like birds singing in a tree.
Love tastes like a sweet bar of chocolate.
Love reminds me of a summer's day.

Amy Kenyon (10)
Hazel Grove Primary School

Hate

I am as bright as a blazing forest fire.
I'm as red as dangerous lava bursting from a volcano.
Are you afraid of me?
You should be because I am a murderer!
If you touch me you shall die from electric shock.
If you eat me you shall taste rotten apples.
If you go near me you shall smell the foul odour of rotten apples.

Andrew Johnson-Hill (10)
Hazel Grove Primary School

Hatred

Hate feels tight and tense,
As pointy as a garden fence,
As vicious as a hungry fox,
As ragged as a tattered box.

Hate is as strong as poisonous blood
And as sloppy as dripping mud.
Hate is mean and very unkind,
Mischievous, with a cunning mind.

Hate is as black as midnight skies,
With evil, staring, deep, dark eyes.
Shows no emotion and does not care.
With a growling mouth
And rough, stiff hair.

Filling the world with lies and bad things,
Shadows and darkness hatred then brings.

Louisa Wood (10)
Hazel Grove Primary School

Sadness

I don't look like anything at first,
But when I'm seen
I turn mean and into
A dark valley of rats.
I'm the jet-black that darkens the night
And I smell of thunderous burning animals on a fire.
I feel pain that make me think
I've been stabbed in my foot.
Petrol stations blowing up is my sound of anger.
I taste like mouldy milk, left in a jug for a long time
And I will be reminded of the spooky blood
Of death that I made.

Luke Burgess (11)
Hazel Grove Primary School

Stress

I'm a house on fire,
As red as lava
And smell like smoke.
You can't stay away from me,
I'm a disease catching you.
I will make you feel as if
A thousand needles are sticking in you.
You can't hide from me.
You can tell when I'm near
For I sound like screaming animals dying.
I taste like hot, spicy pepper.
I will remind you of a relative's death.
Remember, you can't hide from me!

Rosie Spedding (10)
Hazel Grove Primary School

Happiness

I'm calm and I'm bright,
I'll keep you up in the middle of the night.
You see me here, you see me there,
But where am I when you're washing your hair?
I change my colour from red to blue
Because when I think, the sky needs friends too.
People say I remind them of their uncles and grandads.
I smell of freshly-cut grass in the summer.
I taste like a lovely fresh pomegranate.

Mike Wild (11)
Hazel Grove Primary School

My Emotions

I look like the spirit of death spreading through your head and body.
I am the colour of candy apples dipped in red-hot lava.
My emotion smells like road kill in the desert.
Anger feels hot, like burnt ashes.
I sound like a bazooka blowing up a building.
Anger tastes of a sharp apple in my mouth.
My emotion reminds me of bad times in my life.

Callum Spencer (10)
Hazel Grove Primary School

Sorrow Poem

I am a way of apologising.
When you've done something wrong
This will remind you of naughty things.
I feel as soft as snow
And I smell like a bluebell.
Clearly I'm a pale blue.
What am I?

A: Sorry

Danielle Massey (10)
Hazel Grove Primary School

Love

Love tastes like the most delicious chocolate.
It looks like the twinkle in an eye.
The sound of it is a bird tweeting with happiness.
Love is as sweet as the vanilla skies.
It reminds me of the warmness of my mother's heart.
The smell of love is like flowers blooming with spirit.
Love is as kind as a butterfly,
It feels like the softness within it.
Love is the most treasured feeling!

Hollie Hatton (11)
Hazel Grove Primary School

How I Shrunk

Embarrassment looks like a grain of sugar.
It is colourful and bright pink, but it doesn't make you tougher.
Sour pickles smell like embarrassment.
I shrunk into an ant the day I was embarrassed.
Hundreds of people laughing at me was all I could hear.
My lunch tasted of vinegar and beer.
That day reminded me of my first day at school.
That's how . . . I shrunk.

Zunnur Choudhury (11)
Hazel Grove Primary School

Loneliness

I am like a sunset on dark nights,
I am black and orange mixed.
I smell of nothing except sadness.
Loneliness feels like you're reaching for something
And it keeps drifting away from you.
Loneliness sounds like creeping mice feet scurrying across the floor.
I taste sweets that remind me of times me and friends were sad.

Bryony Ingham Tatton (10)
Hazel Grove Primary School

I Am Hate!

I am a black rose bending in the breeze,
I am dark and I make your soul misty.
I smell like a rotten body,
Though I feel like many hateful souls are running through
                                                      your body.
How I sound like moaning voices echoing softly.
Also I taste like pigs' feet cruelly blended with bloody eyes and
                                                      slimy maggots.
In the end I remind myself I'm hateful and cruel.

Jessica Perry (11)
Hazel Grove Primary School

Happiness

Happiness is as yellow as a lemon.
Happiness smells of freshly picked flowers on a summer day.
It feels like slowly moving breeze,
Sounds of a twinkling piano,
Tastes like strawberries,
Looks like lots of children playing nicely.
Happiness reminds you of a rainbow.

Georgia Greaves (10)
Hazel Grove Primary School

Hate

Hate looks like petrol blowing up,
Pure lava-red is its colour.
It sounds like people screaming.
Hate tastes as bitter as a lemon,
Smelling like burning smoke.
It feels like someone's stabbing you in the back,
But you can't see anyone there.
Losing friends is what it reminds me of.

Nicholas Church (11)
Hazel Grove Primary School

Sleep

Sleep is a puffed-up pillow waiting for someone's head to relax on it.
Blue with white spots is the greatest colour for sleep.
Sleep is contagious and will pull anyone down in a second.
Feels like cotton candy, not sticky, but soft and fluffy.
Trickling waterfall is the sound made for sleep.
It tastes like a melting chocolate sensation on your pink tongue.
It reminds me of my great, amazing grandpa going to rest when
he died.

Niamh Clarke (10)
Hazel Grove Primary School

Love

Love is a meadow full of flowers,
It slowly spreads from one to another.
It is a resplendent, tinted, red rose.
Freshly-made bread is its fragrance.

It feels like sand running through your fingers.
Love sounds like a harp playing a melody.
Succulent, smooth chocolate is its taste,
Reminding me of a hot summer's day.

Tonicha Blackwell (11)
Hazel Grove Primary School

Love

So relaxing and a calm, silent night,
The sweet smell of beautiful roses,
The silky red cover over my heart.
My heart flickers with warmth.
It tastes of sweet, great, glorious roses.
It reminds me of happy times.

Jessica Elwers (11)
Hazel Grove Primary School

Laughter

Laughter looks like a smiley baby's face.
Glittering laughter is yellow, as bright as the shining sun.
Laughter smells of a beautiful red rose.
It feels like a hand tickling smoothly on your feet.

Her calming sounds, sounds like lots of cute tiny babies laughing.
Sweet laughter tastes like sugary candy fizzing in your mouth.
Laughter reminds me of everyone laughing in the world.

Megan Pickford (11)
Hazel Grove Primary School

Random

To randomise is good to all,
All sing its praise with a silent call,
Some it makes you not decide,
But it gives you choice when modified.

Yet invisible to the naked eye,
It's like a ball, like a spy.
Random means it's more than one,
Like having a rose and a gun.

It can be wild, it can be mild,
Though gentle as a small, small child.
Some say it makes you not decide,
But it gives you choice, when modified.

Moses Silweya (10)
Hazel Grove Primary School

Fun

I know that fun is tall, enormous like a skyscraper!
That changes form every season,
Like an assorted box of liquorice allsorts.
It's like a fruit machine, my best friend.
It's a sweet, calming, faithful thing,
That's why it's funny and soothing, relaxing.
So whenever you need it, just call on it.
Fun is just like a totally A1 bloke
And never-ending with fun.
It lives in a funny house with everlasting humour
                                        like a comedian.
Fun is bright like the colour orange,
Bright, calm, releasing soothing things.

Luke Ingham (10)
Hazel Grove Primary School

Sadness

Sadness is a light blue colour,
It looks like a river of tears.
Sadness feels like a broken heart.

It smells like a world of blood.
Sadness tastes of frozen water,
It sounds like a tap dripping.

Sadness reminds me of my
Great, great grandad dead.

Brandon Forsyth (10)
Hazel Grove Primary School

Love

Love is calming, it keeps you bright.
In the night it keeps you tight,
And the baby pink movement of the pounding heart,
With the movement of the softly playing harp.

As the gorgeous smell of sparkling roses,
It feels like a new bed quilt with spreading rose petals all over,
And then it reminds you of a pink candle burning bright!

Elizabeth Parrott (11)
Hazel Grove Primary School

I Am Friendship

Friendship looks like the rising sun,
It smells like melted chocolate being poured into a jug.
Love reminds me of friendship.
Every time I see a rainbow it reminds me of it too.
Friendship feels like love.
It sounds like the clattering waves in the wide open sea.
Fairy cakes taste of friendship.

Chloe Hall (10)
Hazel Grove Primary School

Darkness

Darkness looks like a pitch-black rose,
The colour is as black as a panther,
It smells like fresh air.
Darkness feels like nothing, just air.
Darkness whistles through the night.
Darkness tastes like good freshness.
Darkness reminds me of when I'm in bed
But remember, darkness watches you at night.

Lucy Potter (10)
Hazel Grove Primary School

Friendship

Friendship looks like a beautiful animal who is as sweet as sugar.
Friendship is all the colours of a never-ending rainbow.
It smells like freshly-baked, smooth, sweet cookies.
Friendship feels like a kitten's soft, silky fur.
It tastes like hot bubbling chocolate after a freezing cold winter day.
Friendship sounds like a calming, slow lullaby.
Friendship reminds me of a glowing, baby-blue waterfall
                                                that's everlasting
Because friendship never ends.

Emily Barnett (10)
Hazel Grove Primary School

Pain

I am dark red.
Gloomy alleyways is what I look like.
I smell like a burning pot of ash.
I am a silent wind getting louder.

Rose thorn stuck in your heart is me,
I tastes like a hot, spicy pepper,
Sneaking around everyone.

Katherine Parrott (11)
Hazel Grove Primary School

Jealousy

I don't look like anything.
I change every time something sees me.
I am dark purple with the essence of black,
Strongly smell of hatred and death.
We are a modern disease and sound like creeping rats.
I taste of anger and blood.
I remind people of evil.
Tempting you!

Ashby Nelson (10)
Hazel Grove Primary School

Christmas Eve

It was Christmas Eve when . . .
Snow was glistening in the moonlight,
Children were scuttling towards relatives as they arrived,
Parents started to worry as they did last minute shopping,
Children were agitated as they remembered
Santa likes sherry and not gin.
Bells started to jingle as Santa was coming near.
Crunching of juicy orange carrots left for the reindeer.
Rustling of the tightly-wrapped presents as stockings received them.

Hattie Brooks-Davies (11)
Hursthead Junior School

The Big Red Tractor

Driving to the field,
Big wheels rolling round,
The big red tractor roars,
More work must be found.

Filling in big holes,
Shifting piles of dirt,
Carrying tons of mud,
The farmer sweats in his shirt.

Collecting all the hay
In the summer sun,
Chopping as we go,
This really is great fun.

The big red tractor's tired,
He wants to go to bed.
He is brown and covered in mud
When he should be shiny red.

Eloise Jepson (8)
Hursthead Junior School

Dreaming

I dream to fly across the sky,
I dream to fly across the moon,
I dream to fly across the sun,
I dream to fly any day, any day just fly!

I dream to swim the deepest ocean,
I dream to swim the largest lake,
I dream to swim the smallest stream,
I dream to swim any day, any day just swim!

I dream to climb the tallest mountain,
I dream to climb the tallest hill,
I dream to climb the fattest fell,
I dream to climb any day, any day just climb!

Alice Godridge (9)
Hursthead Junior School

The Graveyard

The graveyard in my town is black and misty.
The grass is frozen and the flowers are dead.
Shadows are everywhere, black and glossy.
I get scared and haunted as the wind
Sweeps across my face like a ghost crossing my path.
The church bell rings! I run back home,
Leaving footprints in the icy grave,
A trace of where I was.

Grace Byrne (10)
Hursthead Junior School

Caramel

My pup is called Caramel,
He makes a horrid sound,
But he is cute and funny
And makes me laugh out loud.

He's a golden retriever,
He is full of love and licks,
I have to wash my face a lot,
At least ten times a week.

I take him for a walk,
Especially when it's sunny,
But when it's raining and it's cold
I leave the job for Mummy.

He's very good with people,
He doesn't bark or growl,
But when you tickle his tummy,
His tail beats at 100 miles per hour.

He is my friend,
I love him like no other,
But I would just like to say,
I do still love my mother.

Lauren Sampson (7)
Hursthead Junior School

My Puppy, Charlie

My puppy is called Charlie,
He is only six months old,
He can be very naughty
And doesn't do as he is told.

He's big, black and fluffy
And has great big paddy paws,
And when he is sleeping on my knee
He lets out a great *big* snore.

Holly Henderson (8)
Hursthead Junior School

Cheerleading

C heerleading is lots of fun
H olding my pompoms as I cheer and run
E very Tuesday I go with my friends
E ndless fun, right up till the end
R ed, blue and white are the colours we wear
L eaping and jumping with ribbons in our hair
E nergetic and enthusiastic is how I feel
A rms out ready to do the perfect cartwheel
D ancing and moving to the sound of the beat
I mpossible the stunts look, then I land on my feet
N ew are the costumes, I can tell by the smell
G oing cheerleading with my friend is so swell.

Mya Mannion (10)
Hursthead Junior School

Love

Love is a bright glossy red.
It smells like roses in a garden.
Love tastes like strawberry chocolate.
It sounds like a human heart beating,
It feels as smooth as petals on a flower,
It lives in the hearts of two people.

Love is a bright sparkling blue.
It smells like yummy bread.
Love tastes like cooked, smoky meat.
It sounds like an enormous aeroplane shooting by,
It feels like a little kitten rubbing around you.
Love lives in the blue sky.

Mya Bhatt (10)
Hursthead Junior School

A Winter's Day

I woke up when my mum gave me a soft shake,
I looked outside at the snow, a snowman I would make.
I jumped out of bed and put some clothes on,
I tried to find my gloves but could only find one.
I ran downstairs and put on my coat
And skipped out to feed my horses with hay and oats.
The sun was just rising above the hill
And the cold winter weather gave me a chill.
I could see tall bare trees everywhere,
Whilst the strong breeze blew back my hair.
I went into town to buy some sweets
And when I got back my mum had got me some treats.
First was a book, all shiny and new,
And the other was a wooden doll stuck together with glue.
I ran back in the fields to play,
Then in the corner of my eye, up in the sky was Santa in his sleigh.
I was tired as it was now quite late,
I quickly made a snowman that looked great.
Later that night I curled up in bed,
I soon fell asleep and relaxed my sleepy head.
I did not move or make a sound,
For I was dreaming of Santa on his magical journey, flying around.

Hannah Steele (9)
Hursthead Junior School

Snore

My dad is kind and generous
But there's something he can't cure,
Cos when he goes to bed at night
You can really hear him snore.

The cat is really petrified
Cos in the dead of night,
He comes in from the garden
And it gives him quite a fright.

At least we're safe from burglars
They won't come to our home,
Cos when they think it's quiet,
The snoring's a loud drone.

Mum says it's like a roadside drill
Her nerves are tender and very shrill,
She says she'll stuff a pillow over his head
Then at least she'll sleep in a nice quiet bed.

But I don't care too much
That it's noisy in our house,
Cos I bang in my earplugs
And can't even hear a mouse.

Jenny Bartlett (9)
Hursthead Junior School

My Daft Dad

My dad is my buddy,
We're really quite a two,
He comes everywhere with me,
Even Timbuktu.

Together we have such a laugh,
He plays the fool, he acts quite daft.
Dafter than Daffy Duck -
He has a brain like a bird.
Dumber than a hockey puck,
He's really quite absurd.

He loves me, I know it's true,
He cares for me, he holds me tight.
He always knows just what to do,
When I'm with him I'll be all right.

But when I'm older, I won't forget,
I'll play with my child and be dafter yet.

Alex Benton (8)
Hursthead Junior School

My Dog

My dog is lively and kind,
He barks all the time,
But sometimes he can be quiet and sweet,
So I give him a stroke and a doggie treat,
And when there is an animal on TV,
He runs straight across the room, you'll see.
He loves going on long, long walks,
Up the hill he beats us all,
And at the end of the day
He walks slowly into his basket and falls asleep.

Hannah Hughes (8)
Hursthead Junior School

If I Could Choose

If I could choose, what would I be?
I'd like to be an elf
And have a very magic wand
That I could use myself.

I'd wave it round and round my head
And wish of all kinds of things
But first of all I think I'll have
A pair of glittery wings.

I'll wish my mum something nice,
Perhaps a new pink chair,
And dad should have a motorbike,
Yes, everyone should share.

I'd like to wish something for you,
I know just what you'll like!
Not a watch or a railway train,
Just a clean new bike.

Luke Fallon (8)
Hursthead Junior School

My Dog

I have a dog that is crazy,
I have a dog that is jolly,
I have a dog that has long fur,
I have dog that is bouncy,
I have a dog that is my best friend.

I have a dog that is cuddly,
I have a dog that is playful,
I have a dog that wags his tail,
I have a dog that is lively,
I have a dog that is mad,
Can you guess his name?
It's Scooby-Doo!

Rachael Casnello (8)
Hursthead Junior School

My Nanna

My nanna always opens the door with a great big smile,
She makes me the best cup of tea and we chat for a while.
Her eyes are wide and as blue as the sky,
Has hair as white as the clouds way up high.
She has wrinkles on her face but doesn't look old,
And has some of the most amazing colourful socks so her
                                                     feet don't get cold.
When she kisses my face she has the most gentle touch,
I love my nanna so very much.

Grace Mannion (8)
Hursthead Junior School

Shopping

There's different types of shopping
That different people like,
That includes myself - a truly different type.
Now here's a clue as to what I like
And what other little girls might.
They say we're made of sugar and spice
And like to have all things nice.
Can you guess? Can you see?
It's the place where all the women will be.
Lots of pretty clothes each day to blow the boys far, far away.
Now you have guessed, now you have seen,
Trendy outfits are my scene.

Isabella Hargreaves Cronshaw (8)
Hursthead Junior School

The Tortoise

I am plodding slowly, as if I have all the time in the world.
I'm cautious and careful but still a little curious.
I turn into a rock when I'm in danger -
Not a head or a leg in sight.
When I'm safe, it's back outside to carry on with life.
I am hard, stiff and I never change my shape.
My shell is a dome with a never-ending but ever growing maze.
I have beady eyes so it is hard to tell what I'm thinking.
I have wrinkly skin, even when I am young.
I am a tortoise.

James McElhone (11)
Hursthead Junior School

A Very Special Person!

I know a very special person,
She means the world to me,
She is my taxi driver,
My blanket when I'm ill.
She is the world's greatest toy shop
And the biggest bank.

She is my washing machine,
A strong shield of steel.
Why, haven't you guessed yet?
It's my mum, of course!

Alice Casnello (10)
Hursthead Junior School

My Splendorous Nana

My splendorous nana
Is always there for me
No matter what
If I'm giddy, noisy or bossy

My splendorous nana
Gives me biscuits with my cup of tea
And always gives me warm cuddles

My splendorous nana
Makes me feel special,
Because sometimes she thinks,
That I think, I'm not special

And that is why I think
My nana is the greatest!

Kirsten Williams-Lee (9)
Hursthead Junior School

Friends

Friends are just what people need!
They care for you when you're down.
What would you do without friends?
You can let them rest on your shoulder,
They're as light as a feather.
What would you do without friends?
I have to say, everyone needs a friend!

Alexandra Templeman (8)
Hursthead Junior School

Leprechaun

L urking behind bushes or beneath a tree
E very person who sights him is likely to see
P ompous old shoemaker, hammering while smoking
R aggedly dressed in red and green clothing!
E ven banging and tapping's not his only pleasure
C rocks and pots hold his ancient treasure
H e still guards them now - just for good measure!
A rgumentative, sour, sullen and surly
U nderneath his appearance, the leprechaun's mainly
N othing less than Ireland's national faerie!

Lucy Godridge (11)
Hursthead Junior School

Spring

I like the daffodils,
I hope you can see.
I like the roses
And the roses like me.
I like crystal-blue water,
Just like the sea.
I like the sky
As blue as it can be.
I like the sun to be
As bright as a bee.
I hope you like spring
Just as much as me.

Sophie Holt (9)
Hursthead Junior School

My Dad

My dad is nice and gentle,
He sometimes drives me mental.
He is great and is my best mate.
When we have to travel far, we go in his car.
When my dad makes my dinner, it tastes so good.
I'll never get thinner.
He tickles me after a big dinner,
It is sometimes a roast dinner.
He is bossy and foxy.
After school he gives me a hug.
I wish I had a pug.
He takes me to bed,
I have sweets in bed.
I love my dad,
Even though he is mad.
My dad is so funny,
You should see his tummy.
He is always going to work.
I cry because I miss my dad
But when he comes home
I hug him tight.
I miss my dad but I am glad I have a dad.
He is sad when I am not there,
But he is glad he has got a good girl.
He is great and I love him lots and lots and lots.
He makes me laugh my head off,
He is so funny, he laughs his own head off,
But I love my dad more than anybody,
He is so nice, I love my dad very, very much.

Jessica Lucas (8)
Hurpshead Junior School

Leona Lewis

Her face is like a sun shining in the sky,
Her voice is like a dove's cry in the water,
Her body is like a child working in class,
Her happiness is the flower dying slowly.

Jessica Murray (10)
Lime Tree Primary School

Rhianna

Her face was like a microphone,
Her voice was like the music,
Her body was the handle of the microphone,
Her anger was terrifyingly loud, like a dinosaur.

Lucie Lyth (11)
Lime Tree Primary School

Dave Grohl

His face is a guitar,
His voice is the microphone,
His legs are the stage,
His body is the stand,
He is one of the best
Guitarists in the world.

Lewis Bright (10)
Lime Tree Primary School

My Mum

My mum, she's an elephant
Stamping towards a tree - me!
Her body as fast as a Mini Cooper
Down the country lanes.
My mum's voice is like
A bird tweeting in the sky.
Her face is like a golden sun
Shining bright.

Georgia Taylor (11)
Lime Tree Primary School

My Brother

My brother, he's a NASA rocket
Flying in the sky after me!
His body is as white as a rocket
Flying in the air as if it was chasing a jet.
My brother's face is like a tree
Calming down on the sofa.
His snore is like a rat waiting for its food.

Christopher Harris (10)
Lime Tree Primary School

My Brother

My brother is a sleeping cushion,
He snores aloud like a rhino.
His face is like a gorilla getting angry every second,
His anger is like a tiger
Getting ready to kill its prey.

Premtim Bujupi (11)
Lime Tree Primary School

Nelly Furtardo

Nelly's voice is a sweet baby bird
Singing in the early morning.
Her face is like the bright sunrise
Rising in the light pink sky.
Her body is like a slim model
Tanning on the hot, sunny beach.
Her happiness is like
A precious baby being born.

Sahara Roberts (11)
Lime Tree Primary School

Britney Spears

Her face is like a microphone
Waiting to be used.
Her voice is like a robot
Speaking really slow.
Her body is like a toy doll
All dressed up for Christmas.
Her happiness is like a baby
Jumping up and down in its cot with joy!

Katie Baddoo (11)
Lime Tree Primary School

The Honey

My voice is a singing bird,
My gaze is a sweetness from the flowers,
My tears of pollen drop from my eyes,
My breath is fresh like a flower,
My cloak is the jar that keeps me in.

Benjamin Hartley (11)
Lime Tree Primary School

DJ Alex

DJ Alex was like a microphone roaring a song,
His voice was as soft as a rock star,
His body was like a raindrop hitting the ground,
His sadness was like a plant pot
Falling off a window ledge!

Jake Robertson (10)
Lime Tree Primary School

My Mum

My mum, she's a bulldozer
Destroying houses and people - me!
Her body as wide as a Land Rover,
Destroying everything in her way.
My mum's face is like a stop sign,
Always falling asleep in cars.
Her snore is like an elephant's trumpet.

Callum Lownds (10)
Lime Tree Primary School

The Flower

My voice is the twitter of the birds,
My gaze is the glittering sun,
My cloak is the softest silk,
My breath is the perfume,
My tears are the honey,
The bees are my best friend.
I am the flower and that's the end.

Heather Watts (10)
Lime Tree Primary School

Happiness

Happiness is like a summer's day,
Start of the school holiday,
All the excitement and the cheer,
All the adults having a beer.
Every day is cool and fun,
You get to roast under the sun.
All the animals are about,
Now it's time to scream and shout.
No time for any fights
Because here come the bright nights!

Chloe Elsom (11)
Newton Primary School

Love!

Think of a man calling you honey,
Think of a woman calling you babe,
How does it feel?
What is it like?
Love! Love! Love!
Soft and mushy,
Red and white,
Warm and comforting,
Sweet and delightful.
Love! Love! Love!
We are another person,
Our heart is free,
We dance with happiness
And smile with glee.
Love! Love! Love!

Lucy Kelly (10)
Newton Primary School

Happiness

Happiness is a bright blue sky
And the smell of your mum's home-made pie.
Happiness is a Saturday night,
Tucked in bed without a fright.

Happiness is family and friends,
Staying together without any ends.
Happiness is a rainbow so tall,
Staying up there without any fall.

Happiness is the bumblebee,
Buzzing around with his cup of tea.
Happiness is the start of the year
And something that will last without any fear.

Beth Bolton (11)
Newton Primary School

Happiness

Happiness is the sound of
The roaring waves and laughter.
Happiness is a joyful song
Playing on the radio.
Happiness gives you
Confidence in what you do.
Happiness is a cheesy smile
On someone's face.
Happiness is a child playing
In a spring garden with
Lovely flowers in it,
And happiness is a sign of love!

Samantha Brockhurst (10)
Newton Primary School

Sadness

Sadness is when it is raining
And you can't go outside.
Sadness is when the snow never sticks.
Sadness is when you only get
One piece of chocolate cake.
Sadness is when you fall over
And hurt yourself.

Saskia Steels-Wright (11)
Newton Primary School

King Charles Dog

Business sniffer,
Fur licker,

Meat eater,
Fly beater,

No doubt,
Stubby snout,

Dog fighter,
Bad writer,

Big eyes,
Cute cries,

House wrecker,
Pavement trekker,

Flea scratcher,
Carrot snatcher,

Loud snorer,
Non borer.

Amy Wooller (8)
Oldfield Brow Primary School

I Dreamt I Was A Flower

I dreamt I was a flower
Sitting near the lawn,
Waiting for morning to dawn.

I dreamt I was a cheetah,
So stealthful and so swift,
Running for my prey.

I dreamt I was a butterfly
A beautiful as can be,
Sitting on the flowers,
As proud as can be.

I dreamt I was a little boy,
My bedroom was a mess,
That is when I realised the dream . . .
Was true!

Russell Henstock (8)
Oldfield Brow Primary School

The Sun

Glimmer bright,
Glitter shine,
Shimmer wonderfully,
A summer sight.

Sunlight glimmer,
Sharing heat,
Blazing rays,
Glimmer magnificently

In the bright blue sky.

Jade Taylor (8)
Oldfield Brow Primary School

The Wind

Leaves sliding slowly
Against the ground.
Trees waving swiftly.
Crisp packets,
Glass bottles in the streets,
Bins overflowing.
All this rubbish,
Litter clutter in
A big pile.
Rotten bin bags,
Smelly old apples.

Next morning
Clean.
No more
Rubbish.
I was happy.

Sophie Warmisham (8)
Oldfield Brow Primary School

The Wind

It was mysterious and bashed up,
Tugging at the door,
It opened with a creak.
The wind blew loudly.
I took a deep breath,
The window was rattling,
The frame was falling off.
The wind was rattling,
Whoosh-whoosh it was battling.
It came blowing at me
And I froze.

Ahmad Arshad (8)
Oldfield Brow Primary School

The Rainforest

Panting leopards,
Smart inspectors,

Rain falling,
Parrots soaring,

Palm trees swinging,
Monkeys singing,

Waterfalls flowing,
Explorers aren't going,

A swarm of bees
Flies around the trees.

Sophie Brown (10)
Oldfield Brow Primary School

My Teacher

Coffee drinker,
Good thinker,

Us working,
Them lurking,

Mad teacher,
Loud screecher,

Bit grumpy,
Bit lumpy,

Walk arounder,
Bossy sounder,

Walk stalker,
Little talker,

Big talker,
Little walker.

Rhys Gregory (8)
Oldfield Brow Primary School

A Strange World!

Imagine a world
Filled with flying dogs,
Miaowing frogs
And talking logs.

That sure would be
Strange and unnatural,
But some day
That could happen.

Imagine a world
Filled with chatting bats,
Cooking cats
And walking mats.

That sure would be
Strange and unnatural,
But some day
That could happen.

Imagine a world
Filled with edible cars,
Inedible Mars bars
And pink tar.

That sure would be
Strange and unnatural,
But some day
That could happen.

Imagine a world
Where everybody was fabulous,
No cabs
And lots of science labs.

That sounds strange,
But it could happen soon!

Tamzin Ogiliev (8)
Oldfield Brow Primary School

The Wind

Wind is flowing quickly
Around the raggedy mansion,
Smashing the wobbling windows,
Giving me the creeps.
Brown, bright staircase falling.

Black-bronze bats flying fiercely
Banging and smashing
The dusty windows.
Slimy spiders making the rusty webs rusty,
Enormous webby windows shattering.

A hurricane flew quickly as a storm,
A big flash of lightning came in
From the grey clouds,
There was electric everywhere,
It was overpowering.

Here came a horrendous tornado,
A huge bunch of whirling wind,
Destroying everything,
Sucking in the horrific house
And me.

Simal Asher (9)
Oldfield Brow Primary School

The Haunted Castle

In the haunted castle
The black bats are flying
As fast as they can.
The windows are dirty,
Dusty and smashed.
The wind is blowing.
Squealing black rats
Are making holes to hide.
In the tower there is
A huge shadow saying,
'I want to scare people.'
It is hungry.
Skeletons.
The door broken,
Hanging upside down.
Run away . . .
In the garden
The tree was broken.
A knife with blood on it . . .
Dark red.
There are shadows everywhere
Like someone is behind you.

Deniz Koncagul (8)
Oldfield Brow Primary School

Candles

I dream I am a candle
Like a flame of fire
Shooting like the stars
Gleaming in the sky.

I dream I am a candle
Blowing side to side
Polishing the glossy flames
That flow up really high.

I dream I am a candle
Shimmering and shining
Fluttering around
The smoothly-carved moon.

I dream I am a candle
Shining in the darkness,
Glimmering and singing
A lovely tune.

I dream I am a candle.

Shannon Howell (8)
Oldfield Brow Primary School

Wind

The wind was really strong,
Litter bins overflowed,
Wind as cold as ice,
Blustery.

Six degrees centigrade,
Fingers almost numb,
The bins were battered,
Gales.

I was n the park
Sitting y an oak tree,
There was a horrifying waste heap
In the middle of the park.
I finished looking around,
A sycamore tree with leaves falling,
Crisp packets circling round in the cold air,
Bottles turning on the concrete.
The atmosphere was horrible
In the park.

James Telford (8)
Oldfield Brow Primary School

The Wind

The wind is howling like a wolf,
Trees are rustling, shaking all the leaves off.
The boats are on the harbour bobbing side to side,
Making the waves clash together.

Glass bottles are squelching and covered in mud,
The sound of bats scurrying around,
Flapping their wings at the church,
Fireworks flashing and banging like cannons.

Windmills going round and round
All because of the wind,
Green grass swaying side to side,
Turning dark.

Roundabouts going faster and faster,
Turned by the wind.
Washing lines going side to side,
Clothes blowing in the breeze.

It has started to get sunny
And the wind has gone.

Jessica Tandy (8)
Oldfield Brow Primary School

Wind

Wind why are you howling
Down the sinister streets,
Baking me with your freezy, fragile touch?

Wind, oh Wind please stop,
You're driving me
Like a ticking-tocking clock.

You're driving me mad,
Whether you care or not,
Please can you stop.

Smoke smelling strongly
From chimneys overhead.

Wind, oh Wind take your time
So people can stand your pain
And lay outside in rain.

Erica Dook (9)
Oldfield Brow Primary School

Family

F is for families, the bigger the better
A is for doing things altogether
M is for mums who hold your hand
I is for infants, that's where it begins
L is for love, that's what we all need
Y is for you because you are part of a *family!*

Emma-Louise Tweedale (7)
Our Lady's Catholic Primary School

Ice Cream

I ce cream is yummy
C old as Atlantic water
E veryone loves ice cream

C overed with chocolate sprinkles
R aspberry, strawberry, chocolate and vanilla are yummy flavours
E veryone enjoys ice cream day and night
A nyone will love ice cream
M y favourite food is ice cream.

James Toner (8)
Our Lady's Catholic Primary School

Playtime

We wait patiently
For the bell to ring.
Playtime is a time to play,
Chat, laugh, dance and sing.

Running across the playground,
The wind whipping in my face,
Running to tag my friend
At a very fast pace!

Standing around to chat,
Gossiping, girls and boys,
People are playing football,
While the little ones play with toys.

Playtime is a fun time,
When my little brother isn't being a pest.
But, in my opinion,
Home time is the best!

Chloe Toner (11)
Our Lady's Catholic Primary School

Who Am I?

Why am I stood here?
Give me a clue on where I am going,
Or what I am about to do.
I need someone to tell me,
And look, there is an empty street.
But wait, here comes someone.
Where are they going?
Now I am alone again,
Am I invisible to you?
I feel oh so very sad!
Why does nobody see me?
I am blinded by a sparkling light,
I follow the light to where it has come from,.
Look, a party,
But can anybody see me?
Can you see me?
You see me every day
And never let me play.
Who am I?

Victoria Campbell (9)
Our Lady's Catholic Primary School

Slow Snow

Slow snow comes and goes,
Children singing,
People ringing,
Parents listening,
Trees glistening,
If it's fast or slow,
But you do not know,
Look at the snow
And watch it go.

Alicia Cheeseman (8)
Our Lady's Catholic Primary School

Manchester City Poem

We sit in the stands
Clapping our hands,
Singing a song,
Dancing along.

When City score
We hear the roar,
We've all come to see
MCFC.

When they train
They get a pain,
Then they rest
To play again.

Grace Crosthwaite (8)
Our Lady's Catholic Primary School

Beautiful Seasons

Spring is so gorgeous,
Blossoms falling to the ground
Not making one sound.

Sitting in the shade,
Drinking my cool lemonade,
Summer is scorching.

Autumn leaves falling,
The trees are becoming bare,
Autumn has begun.

The glisten snow,
Winter wonderland I see,
Each snowflake unique!

Eleanor Henderson (11)
Our Lady's Catholic Primary School

Alone

Here I stand all alone
In the streets on my own,
Is there anything else to do
Except wait here for someone new?

As I stare at the floor, so sad,
I'm really starting to get mad.
I don't know why, this is for no reason,
Although this really isn't the right season.

I'm still waiting for someone new,
There is still nothing else to do,
Oh wait, there is someone coming,
Oh yes and they're really running.

So now I stand with a friend,
This really is a happy end,
Now I'm not all alone,
Not in the streets on my own.

Niamh Crowley (9)
Our Lady's Catholic Primary School

Feelings

When I am happy
I am definitely not sad.
If people are mean,
I am still not bad.

When I am lonely
I am definitely not mean.
I am definitely, definitely not a . . .
Mean green fighting machine!

Alicia Blythe (8)
Our Lady's Catholic Primary School

My Little Baby Sister

My little baby sister, small and cute,
Quite a little terror but I'll soon sort her out.
I smile at her and she smiles back,
With her cheeky little grin she'd get away with murder,
But I know deep down insider her,
My little baby sister wouldn't mean to hurt you
And that's why I love her.

Toni-Marie Tweedale (11)
Our Lady's Catholic Primary School

Jaws Of Pain

As I walked to my home
A metal beast bit me, tried to eat me.
I tried to break free but as helpless as I was,
The beast still tried to devour me.

Its jaws were as strong as rock.
I tried and tried and tried but they showed no mercy.
I tried to gnaw my leg free but hope just blew away
Like the last grain of sand in a sand-timer.

I stay there cold-blooded when I hear steps.
I think my time has come, but before the steps reach me,
Help comes to my aid.
I live in pain to this very day.

Jamie Morris (10)
St Ambrose RC Primary School, Stockport

Not A Teddy Bear's Picnic

I am trapped in heavy chains,
Humiliated, depressed.
I am forced to dance a dance,
A dance that I detest.

They bully me and hurt me,
I think it is insane!
I dance to other people
Just to stop the pain.

I feel unwanted and abandoned,
Like all the hope is lost.
Nothing can ever cure me,
Life feels as cold as frost.

Still no one sees my pain,
No one ever will,
Yet I'm still forced to dance,
I'd rather have the kill!

In my dreams I'm free
Like a bird in flight,
Running through the trees,
All cruelty out of sight.

But then I'm dragged right out
And back to reality,
No longer like a bird,
And back to the grey city.

Adam Bircher (10)
St Ambrose RC Primary School, Stockport

Tiger

At that moment I felt I had lost all hope,
Aliens (I think) were standing still, watching my every move.
As they watched me I just stood still.
I felt dizzy, I kept smelling all these different smells,
I couldn't wait another minute, it was lunchtime.
I wanted to join in with these aliens,
However I kept hitting something,
But I couldn't see what it was.
It was clear, I needed freedom.
I hated where I was.
I was missing my family!

Abigail Jackson (11)
St Ambrose RC Primary School, Stockport

Pain Is Insane

The pain, the pain, make it stop,
I just really want to drop.
Dancing to me is so mean,
They watch me because I'm never seen.
Trapped in here, a small cage,
Like my owners get a small wage.
I don't even get to play,
Not for a measly day.
Feeding time's a week away,
Beating time is ten times a day.

Dominic Chase (11)
St Ambrose RC Primary School, Stockport

If I Was . . .

If I was a Transformer,
I would convert into cars
Like a barking dog on wheels.

If I was a Transformer,
I would tell the world
That I was the metal man of the universe.

If I was a Transformer,
I would remove my hand
To use mind-bending powers.

If I was a Transformer,
I would roll in the oil
And keep away from the water.

If I was a Transformer,
I would tremble in fights
But disguise in the build.

If I was a Transformer,
Mankind would gaze into my eyes
As I would shred them to pieces.

Michael Lynam (10)
St Ambrose RC Primary School, Stockport

The Seaside

We play at the beach
On a very sunny day.
We build sandcastles,
Kick them with our feet,
Swimming in the ocean.

Jessica Lewis (8) & Kelly Wong (9)
St Ambrose RC Primary School, Stockport

Shapeshifter

If I was a shapeshifter
I would be as sly as a fox
Hunting at night.

If I was a shapeshifter
I would go as fast as Concorde
In the sky.

If I was a shapeshifter
I would swim like a fish
In the reef.

If I was a shapeshifter
I would fly as gracefully
As a bird.

If I was a shapeshifter
I would go in space on a rocket
And be the first man on Mars.

If I was a shapeshifter
I would turn into a car
And speed off into the distance.

Thomas Reeves (10)
St Ambrose RC Primary School, Stockport

The Indian Bear

They catch bus from bears,
They put them in p airs,
They pullout teeth and nails,
Whilst the bear wails.
People come and come
And the bear feels so numb,
In his mouth, in his paws,
They hear his whimpy roars.

Daniel Keeble (11)
St Ambrose RC Primary School, Stockport

The Sparkling Dragon

In my dreams I thought I saw
A sparkling shadow of a silver dragon,
With shimmering gold wings
And a silver sword on the end of its tail.
He had crystal eyes,
Electric breath
And a crystal staff of terror.
The dragon's claws are like knives,
He stands up and glory hits his face.
His skin is made of thunder and metal.

Alex Worthington (8)
St Ambrose RC Primary School, Stockport

Bonfire Night

The crackling Catherine wheels spin
Like a round roundabout.
The sizzling sparklers sizzle like
Sausages on a barbecue.
The wailing whizzer whizzes past
Like a speedy train.
The rushing rocket rushes like people running.
The flickering fountain flickers like
Stars shining in the sky.
The sparkling stars sparkle like metal
That's just been cleaned.

Lucy Sharpe (8)
St Ambrose RC Primary School, Stockport

Sleeping - Haiku

White grass sleeping tight
On a freezing day, things change,
Make me feel compact.

Jamie Bentley (8)
St Ambrose RC Primary School, Stockport

Wind

The wind on the beach sways with the sea.
I see the sand sail in the sea.
The wind is wailing like wolves,
Swishing to and fro,
When I hear the wind howling,
It scares me.
The waves roar like a lion.
No one can see the wind.
The wind doesn't get trapped in the sea,
The sea gets trapped in the wind.
The wind has a lovely sound
But it is cold and sharp.
It could be just round the corner,
You could be trapped in it.

Megan Toombs (8)
St Ambrose RC Primary School, Stockport

My Sister Is A Monster!

My sister is a monster,
She could frighten off the Devil,
She's brought trouble to a whole new level.
I'm just surprised how good an actress she is,
The way she's good with adults around, it really makes me fizz!

My sister is a monster,
She drives me round the bend,
I just hope she doesn't have a vicious vampire friend.
Her tantrums could cause an earthquake
That would make the whole world shake.

My sister is a monster
But my friends would never guess,
They think she's cute and cuddly, I think she is a pest.
But I can't help but notice, when she's lying in her cot,
Just how angelic she can be (not!)

Rose Byrne (10)
St Lewis Catholic Primary School, Croft

The Sun Stays With Me

The sun stays with me at night.
The sun gives me a cuddle when he plays with me.
The sun keeps me hot when I'm cold.
The sun is bright at night.
The sun has rhythm and plays along.

Kaysey Reddecliff (7)
St Lewis Catholic Primary School, Croft

The Cool Forest

Green, thin leaves dancing,
Rough stick falling,
Hard stones rolling,
Fat tree standing,
Soft grass crying,
Thick fence standing,
Spiky twigs daydreaming,
Soft soil ignoring.

Benjamin Hutson-Redfearn (7)
St Lewis Catholic Primary School, Croft

Animals

Animals are sweet,
Animals are cool,
Animals are nice,
Animals are good,
Animals are silly
And every day
I think about you
And I love you,
An I love it just
Like I love you too.

Georgia Hatton (8)
St Lewis Catholic Primary School, Croft

Chocolate, Sweets, Yummy Treats

My favourite sweet is candyfloss,
It looks a bit like fluffy moss.
People say it rots your teeth,
At least its better than smelly beef.
I also like birthday cake
Which I love to specially bake,
But I just adore marshmallows,
They are as fluffy as the clouds,
When I eat them I'm totally wowed.
Every now and then I like a lollipop,
Occasionally I like a can of pop.
I love an English chocolate bar,
But some kinds taste a bit like tar.
Turkish delight I could eat all night
So I suppose you could say
I like all chocolate, sweets and yummy treats.

Gabrielle Healey (10)
St Lewis Catholic Primary School, Croft

Smiling!

I'm always smiling
When my sister's filing
Her dirty little fingernails.
I'm always happy
And my brother's rappy,
But always gets the words wrong.
My dad thinks
He's better than me
But he's so wrong,
He's so wrong!

Connor Beck (9)
St Lewis Catholic Primary School, Croft

Red

Rosy-red cheeks on a frosty winter morning,
A hot red sunset on a hot summer's night,
A woolly red hat on a snowy, frosty day,
A hot volcano exploding on a hot summer's night,
An angry dragon roaring in a dark cave,
And that's why red is my favourite colour!

Gregor Nolan (10)
St Lewis Catholic Primary School, Croft

The Bishop's Bad Luck

The bishop was fast asleep
And then suddenly a peep
Came from the corridor.
Jus ton the floor
There were big rats,
Bigger than cats,
Crawling in his bed.
'Argh,' he said,
He went downstairs
And sat on a chair,
When suddenly with a fright,
There were ants in sight.
He ran outside to hide.
Over the rivers a butterfly flew,
Along with its tickling crew.
They flew over the tower
With a fluffy flowers
And tickled to death
Until the bishop lost his breath.

Sinead Wright (10)
St Lewis Catholic Primary School, Croft

My World Poem

Snakes pierce venom in their prey,
Squirrels burrow in their drey,
In Switzerland people make cheese,
In Australia koalas climb trees,
In Africa leaves disappear down giraffes' throats,
People build rafts in the remotes,
In the forests of Canada there are bears
And in England worms slither through pears.

Joe Burnham & Liam (8)
St Lewis Catholic Primary School, Croft

Shopping

S hops, red, yellow or green
H ow do they make them?
O range shops look so nice
P erfect shopping is Sainsbury's
P laces have great shopping places
I like cool shops
N ice shops should be pink!
G reat shops are green.

Daisy & Maddy Howorth (7)
St Lewis Catholic Primary School, Croft

Flowers

Red is for a rose,
Orange is for a sunflower,
Yellow is for a dandelion,
Green is for a leaf,
Blue is for the sky
That shines down on the flowers
For you and me.

Kate Duncombe (8)
St Lewis Catholic Primary School, Croft

Treasure

Deep, deep in the darkest cave
Of the chilliest forest
And the marvellous maze,
Lies something more fascinating
That all that can be,
The treasures of light for you and for me.

Not treasures of money
Or treasures of gold,
But the baby who lies there
To love and to hold.

The heart inside that body will grow
And shine for all,
Sparkle, shimmer and glow.

So that is the treasure,
The marvellous thing
It's not some jewellery or some bling!

Katie Janes (9)
St Lewis Catholic Primary School, Croft

Happiness

Happiness is the colour silver.
Happiness tastes like chocolate truffle bars.
It smells like ice cream with marshmallows.
It looks like a big party.
Happiness sounds like excitement.
Happiness feels like cream.

Benjamin Jackson (9)
Winsford High Street CP School

Harvest Time

At harvest time I can see, touch and taste
Ripening fruit on the trees and in the ground.
I can see red, yellow, orange and brown leaves
Falling from the trees.
I can hear the *dumph, dumph, dumph*
Of the fruit falling to the ground.
I can hear the farmers chatting and the
Combine harvester cutting all the wheat and corn.
I love harvest.

Charlotte Jones (8)
Winsford High Street CP School

Happiness

I think of green when I am happy.
Happy tastes like chocolate pudding.
When I am happy it smells like bread
Coming out of the oven.
It looks like blooming flowers.
Happiness sounds like the waves crashing.
I like it when I feel happy
Because I feel joyful.
I like being happy.

Laura Stobie (9)
Winsford High Street CP School

Happiness

Happiness is the colour gold,
It tastes like melting chocolate cake,
It smells like food,
It looks like home,
It feels like a PS2,
It sounds like fireworks.

Brenden Macken (9)
Winsford High Street CP School

Autumn Days

I wake up in the morning to a sunny autumn day,
I hear a combine harvester chopping all the wheat,
I smell the lovely refreshing bread coming from the bakery,
I look out of the window and see the vegetables sprouting
                                        out of the ground,
The farmers are sowing the seeds and chatting as they work.
I go outside and touch the grain as it falls out of my fingers,
I pick up a conker and put it in my pocket,
I taste all the lovely fruit.
All the bright colours are catching my eyes,
Like green, red, yellow, orange and brown.

Jessica Davies (8)
Winsford High Street CP School

Harvest

I can see the ripened fruit waiting to be picked,
Tractors in the field harvesting the corn.
I can hear the combine harvester clinking in the field
And the church bells ringing loud and clear.
I can taste the bread and fruit,
I can touch the spiky conker shell,
I can see the colours, red, yellow and green.

Robyn Bettley (9)
Winsford High Street CP School

Fear

The colour of fear is red and black,
It tastes like dry papaya,
It smells like rotten cheese,
It looks like my sister in the morning,
It sounds like a wolf howling,
It feels like a mousetrap on your hand. *Ouch!*

Cameron Atherton (8)
Winsford High Street CP School

I Hate Anger!

I feel like lashing out at anybody who comes near me,
I feel frustrated and hot,
It tastes horrible and mean.
I want to be happy but I just can't stop.
Is it taking over my body? I just don't know.
Will I ever feel good again?
I just can't take the pain.
I just feel so very *angry* . . .

Reiss Bratt (10)
Winsford High Street CP School

Embarrassed Feelings

Embarrassed is a feeling
That doesn't make you shout and cheer,
But sometimes makes you full of tears.
You also feel silly inside,
So sometimes you might want to cry.
The colour of embarrassed
Is a beautiful red sky.

Sophie Buckley (9)
Winsford High Street CP School

Love

Love is red.
It tastes like fudge brownies
And smells like colourful flowers.
Love looks like chocolate,
It sounds like your heart thumping.
I like love.

Imogen Graffham (9)
Winsford High Street CP School

Anger

Anger feels like mad magma bubbling in your veins.
Vexed, you go blind and just see a red dragon
Roaring in a dark, horrible cave.
You get so mad that your red face
Pops off like a can top sizzling.
You hear a large snoring sound surround you . . . a dragon!
You see the dragon wake up and chase you away.
Suddenly you're dripping wet and feel
Like hot chocolate boiled way too hot!
Suddenly you're floating into space and you see the big bang,
Galaxies and planets rush past you to get to their place.
You snap out of your anger and feel embarrassed in front
of your friends.
You go running to the playground that waits for you.

Shola Hornby (9)
Winsford High Street CP School

Anger Explosion

Anger feels like a volcano pouring out lava.
When it blows, the raging sound is fierce and powerful.
It makes your head as hot and as bright as a bright red spice,
That makes you bang out,
'Stop making me angry!'

Georgia Kittle (9)
Winsford High Street CP School

Anger

Anger reminds me of picking on people.
The colour of anger is red.
Anger sounds like shouting at people,
Like Uncle Ted.

Harry Fairweather (9)
Winsford High Street CP School

Embarrassed

I stand upon the stage, my mind goes blank.
I wonder what to do but I cannot think it through.
My face goes red and I find just what to do
But my voice goes wobbly like a wriggly worm.
The crowd is looking like I am a girl
And then I know just what to do.
I feel really dizzy, the next thing I know
I am in hospital, still not knowing what to do.

Crailin Wilson (10)
Winsford High Street CP School

Anger Problem

Angry is a hateful feeling,
Yet feels brave and strong, but scared.
Everything is rough and looks shaky.
It's not just anger, it's rage, mad and temper.
Anger is caused by people hurting me.
I don't understand why,
And all this is because someone upset me.
They should be sorry but they just laugh.

Jason Wilshaw (10)
Winsford High Street CP School

Evil Anger

Anger is rage,
Anger is temper,
Anger is evil
And anger is red.
It tastes like darkness on a thread,
It looks like a devil on a bed,
It feels like a peg on my head,
Anger reminds me of my uncle, Fred.

Alexander Gaucas Noden (9)
Winsford High Street CP School

Happiness Poem

Happiness is a feeling that you want to shout it out with joy.
It feels like a wonderful feeling inside your body.
It tastes like a fantastic, wonderful world inside you.
It looks like a fabulous enjoyable feeling
That you always want to scream it out with laughter.
The colour is a dazzling, beautiful orange,
And red that is burning through you
Because you are having such an adorable time.
It always reminds me of people
Laughing when they are on holiday.

Becky Wilson (10)
Winsford High Street CP School

Happiness

Happiness feels like excited and
Wanting to jump out and scream.
Happiness looks like fun and fantastic.
It tastes like a wonderful happy world inside me.
Happiness reminds me of people
Screaming and having fun.
The colours of happiness are orange and yellow,
Like the sun is full of happiness.

Lauren Tomlinson (10)
Winsford High Street CP School

Excited

Excited sounds jumpy,
Excited tastes sweet,
Excited feels great,
Excited looks like explosions.

Chloe Walton (9)
Winsford High Street CP School

Silence

Silence feels like times we
Remember those who fought for us.
Silence looks like people
Who are in churches.
Silence tastes like when you are
Eating sweets in the library.

Toyah-Ann Thelwell (9)
Winsford High Street CP School

Happy

Happy looks lovely,
Happy tastes great,
Happy feels cool,
Happy sounds beautiful.

Aiden Sharratt (9)
Winsford High Street CP School

Excited

Excited sounds bubbly,
Excited tastes sweet,
Excited feels light,
Excited looks beautiful.

Kyle Reece-Lea (8)
Winsford High Street CP School

Happy

Happy sounds twinkly,
Happy feels light,
Happy tastes sweet,
Happy looks bright.

Ellie Motherwell (8)
Winsford High Street CP School

The Cactus

The tall cactus
Stands in the middle
Of the boiling sun.
With large sharp spikes
Clipping it to the sand,
Whatever the weather,
This little cactus can live.

Emily Hall (8)
Winsford High Street CP School

Darkness

Darkness sounds like spooky sounds.
Darkness looks like bats on trees.
Darkness tastes like burnt things.

James Maddock (8)
Winsford High Street CP School

Fun

Fun is noise like a barking dog.
Fun feels like a wave.
Fun tastes like garlic bread.
Fun looks like school.

Emily Goodier (7)
Winsford High Street CP School

Excited

Excited sounds nice,
Excited tastes beautiful,
Excited feels smooth,
Excited looks great.

Ben Kent (9)
Winsford High Street CP School

Anger

Anger is the colour of a black pit
Never-ending from the top of the earth.
Anger sounds like the never-ending
Screeching from Death, the skeleton.
Anger tastes like the blood
Pouring from the brain of a skull.
It smells like the puke
From a thousand people.
It looks like the fire from the
Sun melting one man.
It feels like the dried up organs of a man.
It reminds me of the destruction
Of World Wars I and II.

Alasdair Smith (9)
Winsford High Street CP School

Hate

Hate is as black as a cat.
Hate tastes like an old pack of chips.
Hate sounds like death upon you.
Hate smells like a frozen pack.
Hate looks like person to person.
Hate feels like your heart is broken.
Hate reminds you of the bad times.

Jessica Hulse (9)
Winsford High Street CP School

Embarrassed

Standing in front of all the school
Reading out a speech,
Getting bright red in the face,
Feeling confused and embarrassed.
Finally you say your speech out loud and clear,
Then suddenly you can't remember what to say.
Standing silently in front of everyone,
Everyone waiting patiently until . . .
I remember what to say and don't feel
Embarrassed and confused anymore.

Hannah Wenborn (9)
Winsford High Street CP School

Sad

When you are sad
You feel like an upset puppy
Who has been neglected.
You wouldn't feel cheerful and happy,
You would feel upset, depressed and troubled.

Sad and not happy,
That's not how you should feel.
Talk to somebody and then
You might not be sad.

When you're sad
Try not to be,
Forget all the bad stuff
And then you'll be me.

Alexandra Butler (10)
Winsford High Street CP School

Love

Love's colour is like the first red rose just bloomed.
Love sounds like a heart beating softly.
Love tastes like a sugary sweet.
Love smells like a rose just bloomed in the summer.
Love looks like a red heart with an arrow through it.
Love feels like a silk cloth.
Love reminds me of my first boyfriend.

Eleanor Dale (9)
Winsford High Street CP School

Love

Love is the colour of red-hot, fiery lava.
Love sounds like a bright yellow flower that has just popped out.
Love tastes like a crunchy rich tea biscuit.
Love smells like a juicy strawberry dipped in raspberry cream.
Love looks like a bright red, tall rose.
Love feels like a soft, furry cushion.
Love reminds me of nice, tasty, sweet and juicy McDonald's.

Jake Noble (8)
Winsford High Street CP School

Happiness

Happiness is as blue as the deep blue, waving sea.
Happiness sounds like birds singing the beautiful morning songs.
Happiness tastes like some hot, tasty biscuits.
Happiness smells like flowers and mown grass.
Happiness feels like a soft, comfy bed cover.
Happiness reminds me of my birthday
Because I get loads of presents and chocolate cake.

Matthew Warburton (10)
Winsford High Street CP School

Darkness

Darkness sounds like the Grim Reaper
Closing in to steal your soul.
Darkness smells like a rotten egg
Closing in to steal your crazy head.

Darkness tastes like the death
Of an old person ready to see God.
Darkness feels like someone's stolen your soul
And it's the end of your life.

Darkness reminds me of death
Of family and pets.
Darkness is the colour of blood
Running through your soul.

Darkness looks like the Grim Reaper
With his bag of souls.

Joshua Graves (9)
Winsford High Street CP School

Hunger

Hunger's colour is like a soft loaf of bread.
Hunger sounds like the rumbling stomachs of poor children.
Hunger tastes like a sausage being roasted.
Hunger smells like a piece of chicken.

Bradley Perrin (9)
Winsford High Street CP School

Love

Love is red and so is your heart.
Roses are red and
When you bake biscuits with red icing.
I love the scent of flowers.

Adam Blackburn (9)
Winsford High Street CP School

Fear

Fear tastes like twenty-four
Red chilli seeds all eaten at once.
Fear is as red as the lava from a volcano
That is just about to erupt.
Fear reminds me of the dead bodies
Laid out on the battlefield or World War I.
Fear smells like flies feasting on the guts of a dead tiger.
Fear feels like the body of a snake in the desert
That is just about to shed its skin.
Fear sounds like a tiger fighting with a kangaroo,
Hoping to have a feast.
Fear looks like a tiger just about to pounce
On his unsuspecting prey.

Sophie Duncan (10)
Winsford High Street CP School

Love

Love looks like a million pink blossoms falling.
Love tastes like the first bite of dark chocolate in years.
Love sounds like a song from the top of someone's soft heart.
Love is a colour of dark, dreamy pink.
Love smells like the richest perfume in the world.
Love feels like a huge, silk, soft pillow.
Love reminds me of a big scarlet rose.

Emma Galley (10)
Winsford High Street CP School

Fear

Fear sounds like a lurky swamp monster
Approaching from the murky depths.
Fear is as black as the peaceful universe.
Fear tastes like boiled cauliflower
Served up on a plate.
Fear smells like when people
Smash stink bombs in town.
Fear looks like a lava monster
Emerging from a volcano.
Fear feels like a maggot
Squirming around in your hand.
Fear reminds you of nightmares
Appearing from nowhere.

Reyce Heath (10)
Winsford High Street CP School

Love

Love looks like the blowing wind
Whispering through the tall willow trees.
Love sounds like the slowly swaying
Pendulum on a clock.
Love feels like flour falling gently
From the palm of your hand.
Love reminds me of paper
Crumpling lightly in the soft wind.
Love smells like soft breeze
Blowing behind your head.
Love is the colour of lavender
Bursting into blooming freedom.
Love tastes like icy cold water
On a frosty winter morning.

Layla Rigby (9)
Winsford High Street CP School

Love

Love is the colour of a bunch of roses when they are blooming.
Love sounds like the ocean when it is its calmest.
Love tastes like the first bite of chocolate in weeks.
Love smells like the scent of some roses in the summer.
Love looks like a beautiful butterfly.
Love feels like the most beautiful thing in the world.
Love reminds me of my cats when they are very fluffy.

Joshua Rosenberg (10)
Winsford High Street CP School

Darkness

Darkness is as silent as a person with so much fright.
It reminds me of being scared of monsters in bed at night.
Darkness has an enemy, his name is called Light.
At the end of the day they always have a big angry fight.

Callum Coggin (9)
Winsford High Street CP School

Happiness

Happiness is as gold as a golden medal
That would win first place in a competition.
Happiness sounds like a beautiful bird
That sings itself to sleep.
Happiness tastes like a colourful cake
That has just come out the oven.
Happiness smells like pancakes in the morning.
Happiness looks like the sun shining.

Caitlin Casselden (9)
Winsford High Street CP School

Love

Love is soft pink
Like a fluffy teddy.

Love is sweetly tiny
Like a drop of perfume.

Love is a warm heart shape
Like a heart-shaped cushion.

Love is delightfully cosy
Like a woolly bobble hat.

Love is amazingly musical
Like a softly strummed harp.

Love is deliciously fruity
Like a large juicy mango.

Love is supremely sugary
Like a stick of Blackpool rock.

Love is soothingly calm
Like sunbathing on the beach.

Amelia Penn (10)
Wrenbury Primary School

Sadness

Sadness is dark blue
Like a winter's sky at midnight.

Sadness is a giant circle,
Like a rolling bowling ball.

Sadness is extremely small
Like an ant running around our kitchen floor.

Sadness is very slow
Like a tortoise - a slow moving reptile.

Sadness is deafeningly loud
Like a speaker too close to your ear.

Amy Hill (9)
Wrenbury Primary School

Love

Love is bouncy, cool and perfumed
Like a summer's day abroad.

Love tastes sweet, delicious and nourishing
Like the first bite of a freshly-picked apple.

Love is slow and moving,
Like watching a graceful swan glide across the water.

Love is soft, romantic and melodic,
Like listening to classical music.

Love is small and ever-growing,
Like a story made by me.

Love is a fancy heart shape,
Like an elegant restaurant on Christmas Day.

Love is a happy, vibrant red,
Like the Valentine's card from your friend.

Hayley Harman (11)
Wrenbury Primary School

Love

Love is extremely huge
Like the entire universe.

Love is a soft, round heart
Like a Haribo sweet.

Love is sugar sweet
Like a brand new lolly.

Love is bright red
Like a letterbox.

Love is smooth and cuddly
Like the texture of a soft toy.

Love is perfectly lovely
Like the smell of chocolate.

Love is slow and romantic
Like the action of a ballerina.

Love is quiet and gentle
Like the sound of a violin.

Ted Shakeshaft (10)
Wrenbury Primary School

Laughter

Laughter is shimmering orange
Like a sweet peach.

Laughter tastes like an exploding new food,
Like lip-licking candy.

Laughter's texture is fluffy and smooth
Like a soft feather.

Laughter's shape is a bright star
Like the blazing sun.

Laughter's size is wobbly and long
Like wiggling jelly.

Laughter's sound is a jingling song
Like the bells on Santa's sleigh.

Laughter's smell is brilliant and fizzy
Like lovely lemonade.

Jemima Crawley (10)
Wrenbury Primary School

Love

Love is a beautifully perfumed smell
Like purple lavender.

Love is a brilliant red
Like a shining ruby.

Love is a huge size
Like a vast blue sky.

Love is a huge pulsing heart
Like a flashing heart-shaped stroboscope.

Love is a floating soft movement
Like a cloud floating across the sky.

Love is a romantic sound
Like a golden harp.

Love tastes sweet and milky
Like heart-shaped fudge.

David Rowley (9)
Wrenbury Primary School

Anger

Anger is fiery red
Like a red-hot poker.

Anger is horribly loud
Like gunfire.

Anger is burningly scorching
Like a house on fire.

Anger is tremendously spicy
Like a black chilli pepper.

Anger is sharp and pointy
Like a razor blade.

Anger is monstrously huge
Like an elephant.

Anger is rapid and punchy
Like a professional boxer.

Anger is gritty and cold
Like broken glass.

Joe Mason (10)
Wrenbury Primary School

Happy

Happy is slightly salty
Like the never-ending sea.

Happy is light yellow
Like a tangy lemon.

Happy is strongly perfumed
Like the scent of a rose.

Happy is a round circle
Like a beach ball.

Happy is velvety-soft
Like a baby's skin.

Happy is extremely large
Like an elephant.

Happy is gracefully harmonic
Like a group singing.

Happy is fast spinning
Like a spinning top.

Amy Hickman (10)
Wrenbury Primary School

Distraught

Distraught is fiercely white
Like elephants' tusks.

Distraught is terribly spiky
Like a big monster.

Distraught is massively huge
Like an enormous dinosaur.

Distraught is terribly marvellous
Like the fiery sun.

Distraught is slow moving
Like the winter's moon.

Distraught is super rough
Like wrinkly hands.

Jodie Ann Hill (9)
Wrenbury Primary School

Excited

Excited is deliciously spicy and hot
Like a red and weird-shaped chilli.

Excited is temptingly sweet
Like beautiful roses.

Excited is horribly loud and magical
Like giant fireworks.

Excited is a pointed star
Like a bright flash of lightning.

Excited is bright yellow
Like the huge summer sun.

Bradley Williams (9)
Wrenbury Primary School

Terrified

Terrified is vibrant blue
Like a big blue whale.

Terrified is enormously sharp
Like the point of a rock.

Terrified is massively tiny
Like a crawling ant.

Terrified is vibrantly hard
Like a sheer rock face.

Terrified is continuously loud
Like a drum banging in my head.

Terrified is spherically circular
Like the global world.

Terrified is amazingly sour
Like a lime.

Philippa Eite (10)
Wrenbury Primary School

Love

Love is light red
Like a school jumper.

Love is peaceful and relaxing
Like a welcoming bed.

Love is very small
Like a golf ball.

Love is incredibly slow and direct
Like a lawnmower.

Love is really soft
Like a feathered bird.

Love is a huge heart
Like a human heart.

Nathaniel Macleod (9)
Wrenbury Primary School

Love

Love is bright red
Like a fresh rose.

Love is lightly shadowing
Like a white cloud.

Love is a jumbo heart
Like the white moon.

Love is loudly sweet
Like birds chirping.

Love is slowly gentle
Like a baby tortoise.

Love is lightly smooth
Like a fresh carpet.

Love is lightly scented roses
Like a bunch of flowers.

Callum Bourne (9)
Wrenbury Primary School

Love

Love is bright pink
Like a pretty flower.

Love is big and smooth
Like my soft pillow.

Love is cuddly
Like my puppy dog.

Love is a big star
Like over the Christmas tree
At the school.

Love is small and loud
Like a violin playing.

Love is sweet, love smells
Like a perfumed chocolate bar.

Love is large
Like the world.

Ben Woodward (9)
Wrenbury Primary School